Tell me no more and tell me

Tell me no more and tell me

Ralph Hawkins

Shearsman Library

Second Edition
Published in the United Kingdom in 2021 by
Shearsman Library
an imprint of Shearsman Books
by Shearsman Books Ltd
PO Box 4239
Swindon
SN3 9FN

Shearsman Books Ltd Registered Office
30–31 St. James Place, Mangotsfield, Bristol BS16 9JB
(this address not for correspondence)

www.shearsman.com

ISBN 978-1-84861-776-6

First published by Grossteste Press, Leeds & Wirksworth, 1981.

CONTENTS

Tell me no more and tell me

Small lights
come into the day
along the road
where morning shines

a band of music
is rejected and retuned
to talk
too long winded

feathers attract me
and are gone on the beaufort scale
birds flitter against it
lapwings

and rise to your kiss
where a truck goes through
or so it seems
red brick

something yellow in the field
the lane bends
birds again
December sixth

at other times
it is night with only
the wind the hundred watt
bulb and the frosty abyss

alight O monochrome
and take a positive attitude
towards life not one so
self sick though

given to isolation
or walks into the rain
all for the glimpse
of a fox

such strange forms
before me in Italian
but not holding
the bells now ring

in winter
at night
where is that owl
or tomorrow as another day

birds through the glass
I know a row of trees through
the mist and a room of
feathered bed

cars pull up in the lane
quiet faces move towards
a house of wood wherein
if it were not me

and if it did not press
in upon me the gabble of news
the always isolated events
here today and gone tomorrow

I still think of you
as though that helps
all this muddle bathed by time
your letters still on the mantle

I dwell on these moments of
stillness yes I am quiet here

your card came today
and with it too all the things
of habit one day spins
and I make mention of it

snow piles up on the large
window-pane
muddy brown water
bent by the wind trees

where wires spread to extremes
like winter winds across
this marsh
later the above is only

will be seen as the beginning
it is of no import
these taps into the dark
for why

or the pleasures or
the sad removes for balance
of his life and times
reading, reading

and you out to work
being
charmed to boredom
others have energy

right now
water darkens black continues
wind blows
with nothing like no one comes

O little life
where is the way forward
The book on the desk open
the nymph Calypso

when the back aches
the salt sea glitters
and true comfort appears
supplanted in the guise of others

ah the colour of clarification
and the smell thereof
neither can I walk or swim
as geese beckon across the sky

such grey and purple
alas, again, the thought of
in particular someone going away
and returning O the parasitic day

watching through winter the
plain house freezes how easily
comes nothing to be done or
button up the coat this tank

of dreaming water the bubbled
white chemical case with the
birds racing for warmth I cannot
conclude my life here all these

pages and the looks of my friends
one day will glisten out of
January and fasten onto another
you are another and so we huddle

all of us swamp through this
cameo of evening
but that's not this
sight travelling

even social disarray
calling yourself forward
into inter-personal
confusion

ah noise
your beams are light
when I think
if I think

I am radio active
on all airwaves
the march of time
o Ariel swift

you to you I talk
trying to get it straight
for the poem within the poem
also it goes on

only in this
the glint on ice
move a little move
always towards the sun

dreaming the poem
of what
these moments of movement
relaxing into the hour

what vision
abandon vision
or form
or form of action

struggling in days
though it's not a struggle
your friends
in what places

reading the words one
speaks looking into the eyes
lips or is taken on wing
to posters via

a dark drink (poison?)
or the fields now
or what prompted such promotion
without sun's flash

empty day again
you have formed
and are loose on the range
nothing but you sally

forth on a future
still half told
you will experiment
into that gap

these forces gather
dutifully
whilst rooks black chatter
in the falling rain

it is nearly time for
the watch, money for
the supermarket, oil
for the works

yes it comes back to
that finally with an
effort to unfold with
clarity this subject matter

white sheets flapping
of indian cotton
the present voice looped
back to the first line

Bruckner
a building going up
a barn of white wood
green canvas

birds in patterns
across the sky and
gone one lapwing
standing from one

window
from the other
water and weak sun
grey skies

one book on the table
"There is so little that is close and warm"
further, individual leaves
yellow brown green

living in one place
in a life today written
67 years old in a notebook
two letters popped

off a polar bear from
yesterday's dream
washed up without you
he seemed to hint

morning
then afternoon
when the water shines
all is white

birds cluster about
scatterings of food
something fails in my heart
yet without gauge

the brain is back with his
fellow on rhythmic path

am at my third cup of tea
and contemporary music
terrible noise, soprano
this black radio

one orange bar bearing warmth
yes you have triggered the time switch
you wander into a haze
and turn into a space ill-defined

if it were this one
I'd be pleased
as now they applaud
three songs of solitude

it appears now I am shaken
and come as another
brightest sparks clash
with original energy

so as a God I come to another form
time avails not
and the first buds green
have taken wing to

and hours in this grove
of leaf and shadow
pray to these domestic gods
power is not to one side

but we are against it
one room with a window steams
only in action do thoughts pay
evoke force now together

keep the household gods in order
most blameless are they
and we in their path avoid
the clear view and trouble not

and if you are not happy
though concern remains
then when I think of you
this as I am given is harder still

has adoration gone
while the air streams
and I am back indoors
filled with longing

preoccupied with the
seconds the clothes in
a heap shirts three I
think clean and the rest

at tangle of wood, window
frame, fence, trees,
chair in perceptive sequence
lights darting as flame

in insert February
go for long walk as
proposition turn more paper
turn chrysalis

fly thin winged
into now grey sky
mid beasts of the air
never

no more blue whiles
put away pages of paper
this time keep secret all your brother thoughts

and winter on a horn of light
is sky full
the ash is filled with birds
as the eye wanders

while the birds stream
what are they
in the distance the trick
of light fails

without you and with you
as on a pillow of feathers the mind
glides with electric borders of
light the light now is green

and I have been taken away,
sea voyage, in my own thought I drift
watching winter leaves much to be done
yes chop wood and the air chills

from the window
water stands and
falls from the sky
the darkness of grey

following duck
of unseen colour
followed by Vivaldi
"cloud over cloud"

inflammation of the back
percentage times time
China, Iran and Northern Ireland
firearms and ammunition

so go the hours from the eyes
the ears to the phone ring
the cold thud of being
up then down

when the excited eyes smile
knowing what is to be done
accomplished as the birds
start and dart again

the cold air swirls
in a moment I am taken
into extra clothes

the clouds mass
there's no good in this
I lack the conviction seen
in others

three duck one curlew
and further black dots
one bird a sparrow looks
precisely fluffy and smart

it's a Wednesday
green sticks through white
I bend a page to listen

looking
is at present
far enough to think

anxious shirt on chair
thin blue stripe, cotton
in mid afternoon
snow falling

gentle arc of sleep
dream green and
black suitable colour
of day passed unfolding

Madison 6235
never mind that
it's late, 1979
the material is out there

queue for the cans
in a Friday exit
the expanse of flashing numbers
the bill and ticket

the mountains echo on the screen
as the snow piles up
but melts outside
a studio of familiar props

one day again
it is a matter of looking
the peculiar emphasis
of these times

all morning rain
laying flat now and still
except on odd occasions
its taut skin ripples

there is sleep enough
with night and the day
is stupid with melancholy
and dying greens

listening to the rain
fall across then into
a mist all this becomes
transportation where

the light comes to a stop
with a blur you cast off
in a boat accompanied or
not you could be reading

or brought back to the
black and gold of heat
rising in fossil fumes
and spitting with rain

what a water
the blue house-boat
white funnel
red brick house side wall cream

brooding
time's small engine you hope
but one day has changed her
name, one season

if I wasn't dragged off even
in conversation
ripples of light and
distraction

immediate events
all this sound in a room
and a white car from the eye
in the lane

two Jack Russells
and on 86th and 5th you
were somewhere else
for the poet

green cockatoos or oranges
at daylight or before
"In the early March wind"
not March, February

cancelling regrets
with the wind in the chimney
it's the second day of spring
and I'm at another drink

tea, yes the footage reels on
of time and the buried emerge
flutter, climb and shake in
the rain, some are not in

the rain, being indoors
but I am swamped by the clouds
their darkness and my
humming the world without duality

I bump into its inmates
sometimes acquaintances
all this is as ever
a matter of approach

which is as constant as the weather
the trouble is the encroachment of escape
I was never mathematical
or of the fantastic

but testing testing
there goes O radiant evening
sparkling and distinctive
two fish are served

the continual birds scatter
what is there now
because the leaves have gone

the log will go too
once more with the light and
colour of
in particular these

present moments of meaning
which escape enfolding or
to tell you of
keep a log book

ash grey and holly
green or the spines of
the books before me coming
indoors or further in

from the pages
across the fields one
green tractor with white gulls
a row of

in the distance houses
and in this house also there is
dust on the carpet
the carpet

the walls and the curtains
are without flowers
flowers sleep in a pot of
plastic design

when the plain rock shines
it is a London red bus
what do I mean
it is late at night

the weary souls wait, bedraggled
and mine it aspires
the cold wind blows
and the boat somewhere its

horn honks
maybe East River rivulets
anything anyway for a democracy
yes O the waves break

nothing but old stroke new ripples
and you are gone and come again
self's uncertainty
in spring's air

small buds, white soft
catch the eye
as does Larry Holmes
and the musical chimes of her voice

re now
she is the opposition
and the chicken waits as a dish
and food instead of words storms the tongue

where am I cold day
surrounding this, slip
into extra garments
stretching the accumulation

where it is only
these voices, my inter continental
shelf and friends
the cool detached

what do I   mean
conjuring mind the ribbon-like
clouds normal as weather itself
tumbling walking forward

"good day" and "hello"
finding this place strewn with
recognition both in
the mirror and

out of it grey clouds
flatter the sky
what is it we return to
with time's sore

if not that, what
white flowers in bloom

anything but the wild rain I am caught between
the way it rains
and the drinks are poured
who is this

this winter long in the making
but now March
oh ancient China
like gull over water

into Vietnam then Laos from the news via wind
a Scandinavian blackbird
and sleep in a bed
where I shall dream I shall sweat

the townscape awaits
o swift bird or swallow
on course now for spring
our May expectant

Half of Goodbye

I Cannot Wait

you breathe in the moist air of morning
everything follows rapidly
as if turning towards the world for
the quick take, if you could rattle through
it towards squeezed glands then all
the rosewood tops would dazzle, in
the mist of a chosen spray hygiene would gleam
with I know what's best for you
a well tested sound
the yatter of how to spend
passing moments
I cannot wait for something to appear
it is mentioned frequently
that our star will not fade too quickly
lovely things pile up on the plastic
stripped and stained wooden doors yawn
to the cost of fossil fuels
it goes well I'm sedated by it all
being well insulated
I'd coat what rots if I knew how
coming in from the world they don't advise
what's out there unless there's something in it

Moving

winter's cracked stones of weather
I'll miss like the coldness
of small rooms

no more weather here it seems
just one more spring
and half of summer

looking back will be
what is forward now
what bends, sticks and is colour

or to the right and left
what comes in literally
on the waves

I can't avoid where the lines go
or the ambiguity I'm
the adumbration of

no longer will these birds sweep the ground
they will become more like
thin pigeons with one leg

nonetheless street-wise
consubstantial
and harmonious with the elements

Bowl

they are not exactly cornflowers
around the rim although blue a dish
which contains pins, brass screws
and tape   inside a cream sky up
the chimney goes buff smoke beginning
to fade with its drift   thus black
tar-like sits soaked on wood once
beach-white but now the new roof's
wall-plate and yet around this one
just like toy cows transcend the bounded
universe whilst we sit under brick, slate
and water, yes water hits the glass
and steam sticks to the bowl
where mirrored is, or so it seems,
the necessity we impart to reflection,
there is no rain just a washing of
milk around the rim of which I move

And Yet

the clearest of blue skies
my finger bleeds
the days go by
by and by one rises to leave
dust hits the trail of our lives
it means nothing now
and yet
dust hasn't settled
these hours go by
sustaining themselves with
passing thought
which only moments stir
the finest times seem self-indulgent
when the heart moves
and the bed breathes
from the window
the whitest frost
who can tell
as I dust the map clean
if I could
if you want to
where it leads
everything is in place
however slight

Further Views of China

Praying for rain before Chairman Mao
Edged with black crepe
Huge birds fly from the godless mountain
Punishment is not shame
Obedience equals understanding
Mao in the time of Deng like an emperor
Chant his text
What to make of each day
Duck, geese and chicken
Confucius once more
The rocks split and the dynasty fails
Boats colour the Yangtse

Two Composite Views of Evening

1.   the calendar of stars in the sky
winter fed the eyes with bright crystal
freeing winds to blow through cracks
or to suck on smoke in the still night
moon clear the spiral of it straight up

2.   still the birds drift, call it day,
and then the evening sky brings the nervous
bat, moths smack up against the torch beam
whilst indoors so many kilos of steroids
heave the recording world apart

You Got Nerves

swallow all the time swallow
try it again
cross-plot their exact position
how far is receiving distance
no slip ups or
you're gonna need a doctor
take that down
swallow

Foisted Arbitrage

all day you have a postcard
a glass of wine
a man on the radio
Canto with "moder" and "fader"
what can you say
fire dims its glow
you take your antibionics
cork number 907059
will it float
the pigeon in your stomach
can't fly

Terrible Vision

colour out the sun
"that's right"
draw a picture
now write this
if I could
you close a door

A Thief in London

the sounds are rushed
few sounds are when quiet
they take me where I am
the ink prints this
stiffly with the fingers
another set of dabs

Now Not Often Available

what happens in this place can be told

woke up again last night and found myself

and told myself that I was talking

of that it was good to be where I was

not alone not afraid and yet gazing into what I

had forgotten out of into such clear eyes which

appeared mine and read love in words tumbling into

voices which remembered into remembering

such care clarity and fixture of sense as though

bidden by elements eternal and ethereal

which we breathe and are given breath by them

are tempered and urged to be betrothed

and give thanks for you all of you

and found myself at last and only looking at hearing

Animal Adventure

turning a sock inside out
                    putting on one's best clothes
          the ones one has on

one goes up what seems like a mountain
              there is lots of frost and snow
          and looks linger of the moon
one should have put on thermal underwear

          one's mind is like zinc
                  where the green is not grass but
      age around the edges
                  where wine becomes a bath
          one can sink into one cloudy night

one gurgles and swallows
                  at going out to
          meet new people

                      looking up one sees
              metal bits glint like
          snow and it wobbles

          one rotates and arrives out of one's self
      it emerges all in one moment of clarity
          one goes for the holes and
                  a piece of furniture

Life on Mars

almonds of meat
sizzle drenched in
turmeric and butter

clouds come back
from where they've been
but changed you say
meaning me
and birds flit
from one post to the next

take a stance
don't just have
poise over the frying pan
because I know
it will taste fine

here comes more rain
darkening the garden colour
with anxiety

neither sex as
tonic love will
answer my condition

so add more spice as
clouds again
obscure a view and
make another

German Philosophy

my if the story would come carrying us with it
the table is wood
the wood is a forest of timber
and we sit in it and eat
you went there because I didn't know where it was
the knives are made of steel
the kitchen is different
it is worked by electric
the river is water power
the wind is the wind in my sails
the food is excellent
do you think so
in many kitchens steel iron and wood lay dormant
animals also occur but are small

Presentiments

one bird then another
crows
and then back in from the yard
put the fresh egg into the pan
energy steams away
our concernful absorption in what lies closest
the colour is a bright bright yellow
she calls to her husband "George"
his slumber is broken
the chicken sits numbed by the prospect of further eggs
the time is now or like a fire in a small cottage
her hair is a bright yellow
the bird flies away too
George cracks it with his spoon

The Fifth Continent

and it is evening going
up with smoke
as it curls above
it spirals and is
blown smell and colour
as words come up to your mouth
as tea and coffee
spiral up in price
and in (there's a gap to fill)
spite of the approaching cold
the tomatoes are still there
on the vine red set against
green and brown
in their tins with dark labels
in three sizes from
five continents
your ears pick up the voices
where you imagine it's all
different I call you from
the fifth continent
what's the time
it is here time
yes they are still here
there goes once around the light
a mosquito
say that
a mosquito
now say this from
the top of the Empire State Building
a small gnat is flying
it is like flying a kite
keeping all this up in the air

Relaxation

What does one do on a river but row planning further contact with the exterior world. Yes, truly, you're smelling that right now as it comes in with the appropriate season. Oh, it's sweet here you acknowledge as the weather blows unkindly through you into another change of dress. One thinks of retirement, looking forward to the prospective splendid array of gloxinias, gardenias, geraniums and begonias. Never mind where birds scoot or doves settle, where nations rise and fall. This then would be how you live and not where you live. Faced by the round of diurnal routes, dismissing the cosmic array, its splendour, you can muse on what is in the water or as to what objects of glass or stone shall bedeck the mantle. Here, pausing for thought, not breath or sidelong looks, one would do well to note the extremes of other climes with reference to on-going political situations. Thought is always struck down by "what can I do" and annual arrangements are made for cosmetic skin tincture via a travel agent. The dictum is plain enough not to latch onto it, "the interior consistently collides in perfectly placed dead ends". Certainly all the things you admire about the wash of temporal events are not all engaging. One doesn't have to put up with, like our house companion the spider, autumnal insect invasion. We just have to keep the frontage up and walk through distracting social noise, the requests for money, gold-bars, bricks, the pleas for aid from some summary quarter, when you want to look at credentials and not well trained facial expressions. This then is educative; if the drift is not continental what is it? What are all these pieces of pipe in all colours doing leading down to the sea which should be a place for fish and ornamental boats. Here, on coastal resorts, our drabness is on show. Yes, you say, you often wonder about the everyday, exactly how do you see what you do compared say to the idle chatter of ducks on a pond or on inland waterways. What would you do in the face of such horrors (which have of necessity been excluded), those horrors of which you are afraid, or, on the other hand, of what, be it the radiant now or the mirage future, you hope to achieve.

As He Lay in a Meadow

Arising and walking as from benumbed sleep towards shelters in summer showers has been a pastime in ornamental gardens. The preserves of border and design. Similar forms hang in the galleries of recall, precise monochromatic reproductions. Our own walls reveal the stained patches of split emulsion, crumbling plaster and the roof the solar panel onto the sky. From the distance of deep-space our landscape has changed but little where animals, now lost and not seen, and so never present, stroll towards an ash, once buoyed up, but now gone. We know this because we are at times attuned to view the many manifestations of the presentation of being. Remarkably, one has both good and bad days. I can hear it all so clearly, being aroused at night by transcendental visitation, knowing, "I am pottering around in the garden". Yes, the season's spine has snapped where leaves are left upon the earth from French plantings. There is also that voice of indifference, and a voice too which arises from dark protest, a voice bent on reading signs, the particular growth patterns of fungi, the flight of birds, broken twigs and flattened grass. Nonetheless, it is the voice of reproduction. It is called the future and it is the future which evolves from the recorded past in the form of cans and chipped plates of denuded enterprise, what Auden terms History. No one without the faculty of vision would plant a tree, unless a tree of rapid growth-rate, the willows or poplar, in order to have a heightened sense of immediate satisfaction. These trees in parks at eventide when caught in slight but sudden breezes give rise, by way of the interaction of leaves, to a form of anxiety, akin, you may find, to the anxiety felt in country lanes or inner-city covered walkways. Is it I wonder related to the phenomenon of the quick glimpse? When you want that glimpse to be of, to be so especially your favoured E, X or Y. But it inevitably turns out to be some shape inherent in wood or more likely a wood pigeon. This glimpse also occurs on a global scale and is the function of deliberate distort. This in turn ensures that such vision is of an aggressive nature. Vision establishes a vast iconographic technology in order to sanctify itself. This in turn is called, "defending people through scientific means" and has much to do with space exploration, inter planetary invasion and body snatching. For it is said in a number of books, which bind whole peoples to the sky (that my Prince will come), that in a special light, perhaps the milk-blue of dawn, when the movement of day begins and the creatures of night do an about face, one will, if graced, hear the rumblings of visitation, the opening of doors, the inflation of air-cushions. And the stars, one or two will still be visible, preferably the mother planet, will twinkle through a forest of firs in a coolly oxygenated air. Here those of a listening nature will stand staring at the obstacle before them. Impaired vision here is surely grand and always dangerous. For on a smaller scale the engines of the landing craft throb in one's own back garden.

The Colours He Came to See

Every morning he would walk out to look at the buildings. It was quite easy to imagine other places as he walked. The countryside for example in a contemporary setting of boats in a creek. However, the thought of buildings gave him relief from tedium, in the same way as did a well-fashioned oak tree. It was strange to him not to know the dates attached to these substantial entities, although of course he could intuitively guess. He often guessed, not imagined and guessing pleased him. He guessed of a natural kingdom and this implied a qualitative past and not a resplendent future. Blotting out the unpleasant never crossed his mind but like everyone else he suffered from minor imbalances now and again. "It isn't my concern", he thought as he read of contemporary shifts of power, and in the same way he subjected himself to stained glass or the careful avoidance of the environmentalist's nightmare. Dogs should be kept in their proper place. Slowly he became attracted to space exploration, seeing in it a guide to the past, wondering if on previous occasions of exploration what was found to be of worth. He documented the packaging of fast food, the designs of postage stamps, the fashionable young and the expanse of caravans. Buildings to him were the sum of their buoyed up materials. He longed to be able to study the details of their interiors, the fixtures and fittings. In the same vein he noted that material is deposited from some behind or past in various forms and for no doubt various reasons, usually in haste and retreat from somewhere and someone (tangible if in the microcosm in the form of a lover, a sweetheart or sexual companion). When these notions become interstellar then one is stuck with them for more than, and different to what could ever be described as a day. Are you ever the same person? Thus he especially came to view particular colours in a certain light. He was attracted by them and likewise one can see in them his attraction to them: peppermint pink, orchid, gold apricot, sky blue, pale peach, pomegranate, iridescent salmon and olive green. They are all warmly mediterranean and attached to something other than a room or what is offered to a room in silk gloss or matt emulsion. These interiors are what attract him so much, the fact that most of them will remain unknown to him. These buildings crop up everywhere, the ones one wants to enter and cannot. Here time hinders accomplishment and ticks away in a small photograph or snapshot he keeps in his wallet. Like many of us he does not have to look at the picture to know what it looks like. It comes to mind adjacent at various homes. He can go into a room in any building and find a bureau drawer which contains mementoes of his past. Each encountered building provides thoughts of heady dematerialisation, self transportation and passing moments.

Cattle

from this range it all goes out with becoming
naming the objects as they occur
especially if they are black and white the colour of cattle
but, it's all packed meat and goodbye

hello to what's inside this outside and vice versa
mincing the chicken with pork, adding cream,
cloves, mace and plenty of seasoning
skipping to you in a blue dress

"I can read your mind" he said
somewhere in Cambridgeshire potted in the earth like
treasure trove lies our future
when they mean theirs

now eat your meat like a good thing
before hairs turn on my palm or I wither on
some cliff face like a whale I've turned up on some beach
plutonium the colour and texture of a pork terrine

Fish

the one I ate was a buried fish
all day some wires stuck up from a plate
white wires you said in the sun's mugginess
training the tongue in my mouth to say Czechoslovakia

not a soul would come to what was in
half a mile of the place
all day I was left there and am with the flies
perhaps they go about the fish

how do they buzz and the pre-war grater grate
by dropping the tongue to its telling place
the nutmeg heaps by hand
exactly thumb and forefinger

I drive off like a golfer
over a cup of tea the paper spotted
it's all about distance and survival
dust, wind and flare

it's to do with each day
the planes on Nato exercise fly a little lower
they blame the weather on volcanic dust
the fish was tasteless

I roll the ball home like each letter
what's after this I always ask
reversed, the line of trees the setting linnet
in our hive the summer stinks of people

down wind of them you have your preference
the waves slap against the vehicle of moving
it has gone to fat
its tub sticks out at me from the mirror

Birds

sparrows pitch at the wooden walls
there are trays of these things for us on
shelves and behind refrigerated doors
chocolate, malt, apples, beer, yams

I wouldn't think there was any question of choice
as they smack up against the glass
I watch the feathers fly
it's all pennies from your pocket

being told to drink this you'll look good
for a packet of Kellogg's this is quite remarkable
just like peering over a pan at the meat
add white wine, lemon zest and later cream

in a bed of down of goose and duck
but I'd rather be here over my boiled egg listening
to the sulphuric rain hit the lakes of Sweden
or the fact that government policies are working

that's circa July 1980
no I am not undernourished neither am I wired to
the elements but rather to these abstractions which
fill the house with running water, light

and heat, I watch parts of me fall apart with
the years coming to terms with myself only because of
the others and the others are going out to sea of a weekend
cars pulling yachts trailing people in rubber suits

the well mannered affluence of it all I find ironic

Flies

or they lay eggs in the folds of the skin
white from the bone with whiter sinew
where the maggots home like mother like wasp
to that death light though not waxen winged

stabbing meat flies or was meant to or walks
a cavallo with ringing bell hard bullets of fat
creamy white then over the redness coming to brown in a skillet
for the tongue still at Czechoslovakia in the

Stadium of Lenin dusted with flour with the added aid of garlic
the pinched shallot and Provençal bouquet garni
they will be at it in the dustbin
dumped waste at it like sparrows on the wooden rail

not once not twice the butcher is ringing the till of our
tongues bell-less and digital blue figures
as a thing goes zing dropping dead-rayed by a
cosmic agent out with his mother pre-school shooting

down the customers like flies with far east plastic
now the cream cake has taken his eye
whilst mine has taken the pyramid of beans
spraying them they are red, white and green

Green

Stay Cool

the girls hung about in twos and threes
no one was going to move them on
in the warm night Green touched his wife's hair as though he
had a fork for a hand and had found some false deposit on his plate
"Hey Honey"
walking the Avenue late at night people had dogs
and I breathed for air removing my blouse
it was like an early Manet
rolls of smoke came in over the Queensboro Bridge
and Tom clutched his crutch like jubilee diamonds
"It's hot tonight", he said
the beam of light blazed bright in the heavens
as I carried the file of news back to the office I
could hear Joe Jackson singing "It's different for girls"
I knew the planet would survive
I'd given up flying lessons there is no clean air
the plates just pile up with the fluff
and here all thoughts are lies
she beckoned him to a better world
he could see her waving from the germ free booth
Green caught a glimpse from the window of an isle
it was white and water lapped a
shore full of beached dolphins
traffic went both ways always
the lines are not clearly demarked

When They Build Those Things We'll Take a Vote

how does a girl stay young
it only takes five moments
Martha and I were coming back to the dance
dreary old spot up from the lane
when we saw this something before our eyes
he took out a huge rocket which sparked and stuck it in his mouth
"Well, well, ladies, fancy meeting you two once more"
I grinned like I knew a truck driver should
all his castor-oil was from the Hudson
I aged too quickly that night
"Move over testy" Martha squawked offering him her last packet
of fat free nuts, "Gee, don't the sea look swell"
I went through the gears up to the old farm house
not a soul would believe me until I bang bang on the gate
Green looked at the constable
"You ever taken too much speed Roberts"
he looked at me taking out his lighter called Honda he
turned up the flame, "See that, that reminds me of my wife"
the sky looked down
there was somebody waving from a great distance
perhaps a little flame of light glowed

All Along the River They Pulverise the Bark

I never had much insight
knowing for sure this old Russian was smart
like a Martian I could hear him offer my wife a
"Drink", he said pouring the scotch into the glass
"Funny about the game", I said, "it could have gone either way"
"Games", he said with disdain, "what do you know of games"
I cracked up like a lulu leaf
spitting the scotch into the thick pile of his carpet
I remember Robinson coming in on the wire
it was music to my ears
I could hear them laughing all the way to the electricity board
"The old dear's opted for PWRs after all"
I was flat on my back in the heather Maudy beside me
"You must familiarise yourself with the toxic effects of"
her words petered out as I smiled back at Boris
I wondered about all the other old boys he had seen the back of
"You rat", I thought
but he was there before me beaming in with
"You must visit me in your official capacity"
it rained on the way back killing a great lake of fish in
the Cairngorms snow fell as we climbed to the lookout point I
could feel the toxin enter my blood
the way a cow rose on a hump of wet loam
"Good God Boris", I blurted, "they're a bloody good side"
I remember Maudy unbuttoning my fly saying
"Out you come Jimmy, out you come"
I could see the mosquitoes bat size
and hear the cows shitting the way they do
I was being sick all over the carpet

Knock Three Times

Green removed his coat
he had changed his mind
the daily paper had said enough of yesterday
he broke into a fast trot after a butterfly in
what was known as Teacher's Field
last month they took down the hedgerow and re-dug the ditch
the grass was scarred in a crescent shape
on some spot like this deep in the earth's core they could dump
our living waste
it's no good putting a tin pot on your head
but Green put on his skull-cap and
smoked his pipe as though he hated it
our leaders have their beneficial plans
like some distance from us they weave at the pot of spells
why only the other night my wife stopped eating her food
sure something had come for her like a Jehovah's Witness
Green's phone did a sympathetic bring bring
it was the thought of
to Green
of what she's got on is what she's cooking
he could still smell the olive oil from there

Solo

driving back solo through the air
I had Green's words in my ears
I was in the right spot as though a beacon had been lit
the light seemed to radiate about the thickness the colour
of some chicken dish made from a white roux and the zest of lemon
how I lingered over the stove with the wooden spoon
thinking of her amongst beached whales
the air full of chemicals leaving the taste of burnt toast in
my mouth the fields under the drizzle of spray
"There's not much we can do", said Green
I knew he didn't believe my story
but the papers did I read my name and saw my face
I walked along Lenin Boulevard in late autumn the dipping trees
rocks full of basking lizards stalls full of ripe peaches
maybe that was it I cut the engine and waited
there were other watchers too from bedroom windows Disney
children looked out with smiling neatness
Green mumbled something to Maudy
his head contained a great luminescence
he stabbed at the chicken mumbling about food poisoning
he ached in his comfort dribbling away for his hidden moments
I wasn't sure if he believed in UFOs but sure enough
all along the coast in hidden places
the photos were doctored the water cleanly flowed
and monster fish bathed in its warmth
Windscale was as clean as a germ free booth

Tummy Trouble

the river sparkled
a small collection of holiday snaps drifted through his head
"He was killed by what!" said Green
"Do you remember darling when"
she kissed him in the half lit room
"Bugger the bloody man", said Green thinking of his
steak and kidney he knew he could smell a rat
Boris handed him the envelope of poisoned charms
"You see", he said lifting his finger to his lips, "we have no
qualms about these matters", little did he know, thought Green,
do we. Right now the cabinet is mumbling away about security
"Your food is always so delightful", I said to Boris
I gave Maudy a wink and wondered what old Green would think
and then I felt a web spread through my intestines
"I will see you next week", I enquired
the rat grew bigger in Green's thoughts
but the days were still months and years
it was all routine
calming her telling her of that one day and thinking always of Maudy
he looked in the mirror pulling down his lower lip
to examine the plaque on his teeth
he thought he'd go to bed with just one more scotch
he didn't give a fuck
he'd get the report tomorrow

Rider

I patted my life on the head
there was nobody to wave to
the wife would be home soon from work
I had my alibi
I put all the pots and pans on the cooker
Green flopped like a beached whale into his bath
Maudy with her hand towel soaping his cock
the children were asleep as I put on my spacesuit
rising into the night air I knew would be pretty good
one body re soul was enough for one day thought Green but
two my god he felt the sperm pulse from him as though it were
a thought it was satisfying looking at it with as much
interest as if it were truly a passing cloud
his thoughts worked slowly but precisely
what pleased him once had disappeared into the mesh of routine
he looked at the marriage and the beach photo
he preferred tea to coffee
so he told her when he got to work in the morning "Coffee"
Maudy grinned undressed and stepped into the bath
the water rose up a blue cliff face
Green didn't have to open his mouth being a whale
there was no interference on the network
yet no one cooked a better breakfast than her
he may well be the innocent
I have heard there are good people in bad places
you are listening to a tree
the air keeps it up because it breathes
again she smiled through all the years
like he looked at the moon
she was speaking but they never got along

Never Say Goodbye

I turned green
walking up one road and dashing around the corner
Agnes told me, you remember Agnes, "Go to the *Two Donkeys*"
it was there whilst
just like at Heathrow I could do a quick turn
know each stairway each passageway
"Okay Beano", he said and gave me the Bristol package
if the streets were cobblestone
then I'd know where to go
I could lay eggs in the runnels
I knew every inch like I was Prince Charles' masseur
"How's the dog", I'd say to his mother
Agnes gave me a drink
I could see my wife having lunch with a Martian
it was like a religious conversion going home
knowing I was to die with my plate empty
I was being press-ganged
Green stood there sucking on his pipe dreaming of his desk sergeant
he didn't know I was in my jockey-shorts staring at a
UFO and my wife waving from a portal
Green removed the package from my belongings
unwrapped it lay like a small planet
in the tracery of his future
flat black and biblical

The Coded Spider

I couldn't carry on this double bluff
these ant people were perfect
I'd settle down to be one of their number
no one could tell me what the weather was going to be like
Green saw me vomit
he came from his hiding place, "Hard luck fella, you've just failed"
he wouldn't play back the video
so I wrote down the recipe again
the ingredients never change just the quantities
not far away Boris listened to his last move
all the people of the world were captive to the few who held the final
telex, at that very moment they were taking soil samples
in the Peak District
"Bury him in earth and sand", thought Green, but his eggs were
scrambled because he came out with, "Okay, take him back to the cell"
I loaded up once more
why the sky was filled with dust I didn't know
but life was sure passing fast
with an air-burst they could wipe out the whole of East Anglia
if I had kept my suit handy I could have gone then
maybe my wife was correct
all of a sudden I could see Americans everywhere
Green welcome me at Heathrow, had I been turned
"Meet Maudy", he said, "she's under the covers too"
he didn't bother to correct himself, as he waved he turned
it was my face from the past
again I watched the ball go off into the sky
it was all 3 D
Maudy touched my thigh with her knee
"Come creature", she said, "bury me"

Be Young Be Happy

"I'm not answering yes to your question neither am I saying no"
there was no way of knowing for sure if their scam had worked
everything was underground and covered up
mobilisation would only take a matter of minutes
I watched her dress for the last time
"It's no good", she said, "I'm going"
Green looked at me as though I were a starfish
if only my heart would stop pounding
the times I wanted to hit out
but fish in the sky who would believe that
"Drink or drugs", queried Green of Roberts
he stood there looking at an ancient map of China
I brought up again the fact that she'd been abducted
both their faces became coincident in thought and expression
"Snap", I thought but they never knew even then
I read Green's eyes going over Maudy's buttocks
and here he was doing a clean air act with me
"Thomas Hardy", he said, "Thomas bloody Hardy, that's who I was
thinking of" nobody said he was lying because nobody asked him
there were only the three of us and Roberts was straight from
a backward planet for the rest of his life
"God damn it fellow, admit it, admit it will you, you're
working for the other side"
I honestly didn't know what he was on about
"Do you think I'm going to sit around and starve
whilst you fuckers study your wall-charts"
he'd be one of the select, guided through false walls, drainage
and subway systems, two-way mirrors and time controls
right then I tuned out of any bell he tried to ring
I could see her again with that stricken face
afraid to call for help afraid
Maudy thought of Green and then he flew over her in the final dust cloud
startled he said, "Perhaps I've been on this case far too long"
it was then I made her a cup of tea
dreaming of the years gone and the ones to come

But it may be so

It always rains against the front door
thumb latch
west south west
nowhere the world
her fields all green
drum against the changes
looking at it looking

under the carapace
various concerns
your brittle shell
soft blue to a bird
ducklings on a lake
what make
you out

dash in and out
temperature rising
earth sweats now rain
now birds now breath
in a tumble the micro
circuits of communication
trouble in

if you walk
the wind is high
various insects
various colours
take wing or hop
from what you say
from vetch and grass

or earth
she is
of other worlds
light was
in her birth
room and dark
the fragrance from almond

another
quick
rose
your voice
the door
I mean a flower
with thorns

you are lost without trace
but I could trace you
but no longer in that way
as long as the brain I flitter
brings in what it does
an old no
a new yes

smoking an old cigarette
where
do you feel at home
you wander
with things to do
you put off
are tentative

in the distance the still
moving
the news washes over me
as I glance from that to this
why
I shall fabricate a way both
in and out of this

in the middle of now
in the day changing
the wind
constant
bird talk
animal fidget
I itch thought

some plates are in season
how they come and go
balanced by what the eye
sees and the mind's eye
so it isn't a documentary
the way the fields change
and the pollen floats

you are my slight changes
fully at home and restless
thinking of the electrical
insurgence we are all wires
this month of the longest day
not knowing what to make of
the news, which service

time for a change
heading into the hinterland
got my bags packed ready to unload
and what would you take with you
1 : if you were going to another world
2 : if you were leaving home
3 : if you were going on holiday

pale grey of my moods
maybe not
well, to another world nothing, sweet fuck all
home, the colours of mud, slate of sky
I aint ever got there
all these trees
for birds to perch in

the appearance of food is always important
just dish the stuff up
or Gods
as the big bee bumps into the window
for three I guess a few books
the smell of mint
the red of paprika

still raining
gentle rain last night
and again this morning
their songs never more
various their down
so white their little
ring collars

the words as though
they flake off and
scatter
clinging to a thin
line
sparks fly off
and gel

insular
sleeping under new conditions
I cannot say
you were sticky
but I'm O
it's a song
stuck on you

drift in and out all day
of the light as it shifts
through colour
am I stuck, stranded or moving
and in what
the light shines from a
this lamp

it will not stand still
in such a small place
pictures of the world
imagine what you see and hear
constantly
you will not make sense of it
though you try

break what you say
up into
lemon and herb
the fissure of fracture
the neat and bright speak of
with such surety
give us a light guv

leave the paper in
just in case
and say
I haven't a penchant for mystery
I will try to
path the clear
of nettles

fabric of the warm
materials
yolk swelling to
blood
ducklings and geese
in wind and rain
on water

you dunk yourself in
I hear the water running
the martins over the water
it's boiling for tea
we agree over this surface
the words slide
and are tapped

from the paper
he wanted to play a cultural piano
the way some play with syntax
he didn't know an adjective from an adverb
now you kids listen, ciao
I am not rewriting the Maximus
but learnin to talk proper

wherever you go
your head is full of bumps
then there and now
where would you be without them
is this a temple
no
it's a broken nose

but our luck can change here too
in this sleepy town
of constant or so it seems
wind the flat and few trees
you feel you impose on others
my tongue wobbles my knees shake
why be so silly

then I went
distorting and walking
with indulgence
I should stop this
call myself another
I mean change my name
if this I is I

is this true or false
or too close
what is there to do
you have your own notions
we are entering a thermal
up and rise we go
trying to change

whose voice is this
moving through various waves
caught up and carried
there go the birds
and here comes
there is no place to go
except there (no t)

it is all here
skips of the heart
beat of the words
no mention of stars
where in heavens
June days full of
clouds my clear eye

double fault
precise time
date
season of what bird
flower names of grasses
long light
no ball

grasses pollinate
June the 24th
the clouds
wondering what others think
how all these years
your friends are
both come and gone

the last day
warm air and the
world full of news
between friends
in a small way
I wonder with this
rebuffed as I am

full of doubt
oh he wants no more than
what does he want
in this small town
estranged and hello
brittle as a pun you
come from where you've been

shall I measure this room
a number of friends
in a novel of the marshes
in bleak winter wind and grey
in summer blossoms
at night the fields fall short
to encircle the home with stars

www.ingramcontent.com/pod-product-compliance
Lightning Source LLC
Chambersburg PA
CBHW020214090426
42734CB00008B/1066